spy, n. — a secret agent employed by a government or other organization
to gather intelligence relating to its actual or potential enemies

Spies around the World

MOSSAD

AND OTHER ISRAELI SPIES

Michael E. Goodman

Violence in the Middle East has bred distrust between Palestinians and Israelis over the years.

Table of Contents

Chapters

- - - - - - - - - - - - - - - - - - - -

Evolution of Espionage

- - - - - - - - - - - - - - - - - - - -

Published by Creative Paperbacks
P.O. Box 227, Mankato, Minnesota 56002
Creative Paperbacks is an imprint of
The Creative Company
www.thecreativecompany.us

Design and production by Blue Design
Art direction by Rita Marshall
Printed in the United States of America

Photographs by Getty Images (AFP, JOSEPH BARRAK/AFP,
CHRIS BOURONCLE/AFP, David Boyer/National Geographic,
DigitalGlobe, Stephen Ferry/Liaison, Terry Fincher/
Express, MENAHEM KAHANA/AFP, ATTA KENARE/AFP,
Keystone, Keystone-France/Gamma-Keystone, MARCO
LONGARI/AFP, Ministry of Defense, MPI, ALEXANDER
NEMENOV/AFP, Pictorial Parade/Hulton Archive,
Popperfoto, Co Rentmeester/Time & Life Pictures,
David Silverman, Uriel Sinai, Terrence Spencer//Time
Life Pictures, PIERRE VERDY/AFP, SAM YEH/AFP)

Library of Congress Cataloging-in-Publication Data
Goodman, Michael E.
The Mossad and other Israeli spies / by Michael E.
Goodman.
p. cm. — (Spies around the world)
Includes bibliographical references and index.
Summary: An eye-opening exploration of the history of
the 1951-founded Mossad and other Israeli espionage
agencies, investigating their typical training and
tools as well as the escapades of famous spies.
ISBN 978-1-60818-228-2 (hardcover)
ISBN 978-0-89812-971-7 (pbk)
1. Israel. Mosad le-modi'in ve-tafkidim meyuhadim—
Juvenile literature. 2. Intelligence service—Israel—
Juvenile literature. 3. Espionage, Israeli—Juvenile
literature. I. Title.

UB251.I78G66 2012
327.125694—dc23   2011035792

First Edition
9 8 7 6 5 4 3 2 1

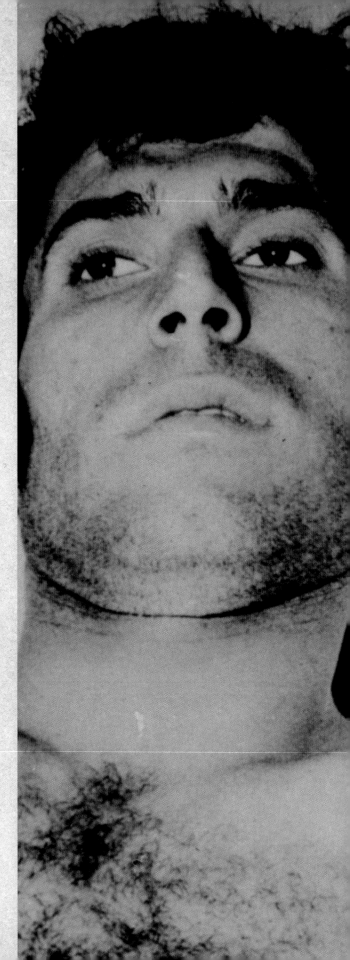

The Mossad hunted down the terrorists responsible for the Munich massacre in 1972.

Only hours after the nation of Israel was established on May 14, 1948, five neighboring Arab nations attacked, hoping to wipe out the new country. The attackers had far more soldiers and weapons than Israel but underestimated how much information Israeli spies had already gathered about the Arab nations' military capabilities and strategies. The war quickly turned in Israel's favor. Israel's survival from 1948 to today has depended on its maintaining a well-established intelligence network to gather secret data, carry out covert operations, and counter terrorism. At the heart of this network is the Mossad, a shadowy organization charged with keeping Israel safe from outside enemies by any means necessary.

BIBLE TO BAYONETS

Espionage has a long and glorious history in Israel. According to the Bible, before the Israelites crossed into the land of Canaan in their exodus from Egypt, their leader Joshua sent out spies to reconnoiter the area around Jericho. The intelligence the spies gathered helped the Israelites to conquer the town and begin building their first kingdom.

More than 3,000 years later—even before Israel became an official nation in 1948—Jewish settlers in the British-controlled region of the Middle East then called Palestine formed underground groups to push for more Jews to be allowed to enter the region. Their activities intensified as millions of European Jews were slaughtered by German Nazis during World War II (1939–45). Jewish groups around the world began pushing for the creation of a safe haven for Jews. Arab countries in the region opposed this idea and threatened to destroy any Jewish state that was established. The Arab–Israeli War that began in May 1948 was designed to carry out that threat.

By the early 1950s, Israel's first prime minister, David Ben-Gurion, had created a three-prong intelligence network to protect the new country from the enemies that surrounded it. He chose a verse from the biblical book of Proverbs (11:14) to explain his action: "Where no counsel is, the people fall, but in the multitude of counselors there is safety." One prong of the intelligence network, named Aman, would handle military intelligence, gathering data about enemy forces and weaponry that might threaten Israel. A second institution, Shin Bet, would be responsible for security and counterintelligence within the country, much like the Federal Bureau of Investigation (FBI) in the United States. Counterintelligence involves protecting a country's secrets against sabotage and neutralizing the work of enemy spies working within the country.

The third prong, the Mossad, whose Hebrew name translates as "the Institute for Intelligence and Special Operations," would have the widest-ranging responsibilities. These would include gathering intelligence outside Israel's borders; preventing Israel's enemies from developing weapons; preventing

MOSSAD

Right: David Ben-Gurion proclaimed that Jews had a right to be "masters of their own fate" in Israel.

EVOLUTION OF ESPIONAGE
The Spy Who Wrote Poetry

In 1943, the Nazis occupied Hungary and began transporting most of that country's Jews to concentration camps. In Palestine, Hungarian-born Hannah Senesh decided she had to do something to help. She volunteered to parachute behind the German lines in Hungary as a member of a special Haganah intelligence unit trained by the British army. Senesh was caught, tortured, and eventually executed but never revealed any information to her captors. Throughout her ordeal, she kept up the morale of the other prisoners by singing songs based on poems she had written. Today, many of her poems, like the one below, are still recited in Israel.

Blessed is the match that burns and kindles the fire,
blessed is the fire that burns in the secret heart.
Blessed are the hearts that know how to stop with honor . . .
blessed is the match that burns and kindles the fire.

or responding to terrorist acts against Israelis around the world; cooperating with espionage organizations in other countries friendly to Israel; and developing covert spy networks in both friendly and hostile countries.

The Mossad's reputation for being an efficient and sometimes deadly organization has been built on the "special operations" it has conducted. From kidnapping an infamous Nazi war criminal in Argentina and sneaking him into Israel to be put on trial to bloodily avenging the 1972 murders of 11 Israeli Olympic athletes and coaches; and from coordinating a daring late-night rescue in Africa of more than 100 Jewish passengers of a hijacked plane to planting spies inside 2 enemy countries to provide the intelligence Israel needed to win a major war in only 6 days, the Mossad has done everything it could to protect its country and citizens.

Like most intelligence organizations, the Mossad is secretive about its operations. The less enemies know about how the organization is run, the better off Israel will be, the country's leaders reason. Some of the Mossad's secrets have gradually come to light, though. For example, we now know that 1,500 to 2,000 of Israel's total population of 7.7 million people work for the Mossad. All are civilians, though most served in the military when they were younger. Most work within Israel, near the organization's headquarters in Tel Aviv. Mossad `operatives` based in other countries often live undercover, using false identities.

The Mossad carries out its duties through eight separate departments. The largest is the Collections Department, which gathers intelligence data sent by spies from around the world. Other departments coordinate planning and operations, `propaganda`, research (especially concerning `nuclear` capabilities of other nations), technology, and political cooperation with governments friendly to Israel. The most secretive department is known by the Hebrew name Metsada, meaning "fortress." Its work, as described in the British journal

Intelligence concerning the military has been the domain of Aman since Israel's early days.

The Heron drone, made by Israel Aerospace Industries, can fly for almost 50 hours at a time.

Jane's Intelligence Review, involves "small units of combatants who carry out actions abroad against those considered to be a threat to Israeli security…. These missions have included assassinations and sabotage." The assassination squads have their own name, Kidon, which is Hebrew for "bayonet."

Although the Mossad receives most of the publicity—both good and bad—the other two branches of the Israeli intelligence network carry out functions vital to the nation's security as well. Aman is composed of approximately 7,000 military and civilian employees. Aman's air force intelligence division operates high-speed piloted aircraft and unmanned drones to spy on the military facilities of other Middle Eastern countries. Israel wants to know if any facilities are being constructed to make weapons to use against it. Aman's naval intelligence division collects data on any naval activities in the Mediterranean Sea and draws up plans for protecting the country from attacks by sea. Other Aman employees monitor and intercept enemy radio and Internet transmissions that may contain plans for covert action against Israel.

Aman's job became both more critical and more complicated following a war in 1967 when Israel annexed, or took over, two areas that had previously been under

EVOLUTION OF ESPIONAGE
Underground Immigration

In 1956, the country of Morocco achieved its independence from France, and a new Muslim government took over. Jews in Morocco feared they would be in danger. Many wanted to come to Israel, but the government did not allow them to leave. In response, the Mossad set up an underground immigration network. Agents provided military and communications training to Moroccan Jewish volunteers, who helped hundreds of their countrymen escape to British-controlled Gibraltar. There, they boarded boats for Israel. The Moroccan secret police tried to shut down the escape network, but pressure from other countries eventually changed the policy. Soon, most of Morocco's Jews began new lives in Israel.

Egyptian and Syrian control—Gaza in the west and the Golan Heights in the northeast. Arab nations and Palestinians have long opposed Israel's control of these regions and have threatened to take them back by force if necessary.

Shin Bet is responsible for uncovering any enemy spy operations in Israel or exposing Israeli citizens who may be spying for other countries. Shin Bet also coordinates with Israel's national airline, El Al, to provide security for both incoming and outgoing passengers. In addition, many of the organization's approximately 1,000 employees devote significant time and effort to detecting, preventing, and combating terrorist attacks by militant Palestinians opposed to living under Jewish control in the country. In the U.S., you might hear or read about four or five terrorist acts a year. On Shin Bet's Web site, reports are posted monthly, detailing as many as 180 attacks in the tiny country in a single month. In combating terrorism, Shin Bet employs many agents who pose as Palestinians and work undercover inside Palestinian communities. Before being assigned, these agents are put through a test. They must go into a Palestinian marketplace and interact comfortably with shoppers there without raising suspicion.

EVOLUTION OF ESPIONAGE
Stealing from the Soviets

In August 1966, the Mossad made headlines by stealing a Russian warplane being used in Iraq. Actually, the Mossad didn't steal the plane; an agent based in Baghdad convinced an Iraqi pilot to fly the high-tech aircraft to Israel. The agent scouted for several months and found a Christian pilot named Munir Redfa, who was openly unhappy with how Iraqi leaders treated people in the country who were not Muslims. Eventually, she persuaded Redfa to fly his Russian-made MiG-21 to Israel, where his family would meet him to live. While Iraqi and Russian leaders were embarrassed by the defection, Israel and its allies eagerly inspected the latest model of Russian fighter aircraft.

Aircraft produced by the Russian design bureau Mikoyan-and-Gurevich were known as "MiGs."

LIFE IN THE SHADOWS

Have you ever thought about becoming a spy? If you watch movies featuring suave agents like James Bond or undercover killing machines such as Jason Bourne, you probably think a spy's life must be pretty glamorous or exciting. More often than not, it is dangerous or nerve-racking instead. If spies are discovered, the governments or groups they are spying on may jail or even execute them. Seemingly innocent mistakes can prove costly. For example, Mossad agents posing as citizens of a foreign country are cautioned to wear only clothing and shoes from that country. Being caught with Israeli-made underwear in an Arab country has tripped up several Israeli spies and led to their capture.

Most spies are not as attractive or as daring as the actors in movies. Espionage agencies look for average-looking people who can blend in with those around them. They are usually of ordinary height and build. Most are also able to speak several languages. A Mossad or Shin Bet agent, for example,

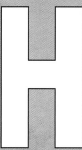

should be fluent in Arabic and English as well as Hebrew, and knowledge of Russian can also be helpful.

What makes people want to be spies—or agree to become spies against their will? According to American journalist and espionage expert Ernest Volkman, the reasons can be summed up with the acronym MICE. The letters represent the words *money, ideology, compromise,* and *ego.* Some people become spies because they are paid well for the information they uncover and transmit. Others become spies because they have a strong belief in their country or in

the ideals represented by another country. Others may be blackmailed, or compromised, into spying to avoid punishment or to prevent some dark secret about themselves from being revealed. Still others may think that becoming a spy is the way to show off how clever or daring they can be.

There are several types of spies, and not all live or act the same. Spies working in another country fall into two categories: legals and illegals. Legals work openly in their own country's embassy in a foreign country. As an official government employee, they are allowed to bend some rules of the nation in which they are working. If legals are caught spying or trying to recruit others to spy for them, they

Opposite: Suspected Russian spy Anna Chapman, captured in 2010, likely became a spy because of ideology.

EVOLUTION OF ESPIONAGE
The Empty Barrels

A Mossad trick helped Israel build its first nuclear weapons in the late 1960s. In order to produce the plutonium needed to fuel the weapons, Israel required a large supply of uranium ore, but no country would sell uranium to Israel. A Mossad operative named Dan Aerbel came up with a plan. He established a business relationship with a chemical company in Belgium and persuaded one of its owners to order 200 tons (181 t) of uranium ore and then ship it to another company in Italy. Between Belgium and Italy, the ship made an unscheduled stop. When it finally docked (in Turkey), its cargo consisted only of empty barrels.

are usually sent back to their home country rather than jailed.

Illegals are spies who assume false identities and work undercover. If they are caught, their punishment often takes severe forms, from torture to execution. Some illegals create elaborate legends, or cover stories about themselves, to conceal their spying activities. Terms used to label illegals include mole, double agent, or asset.

As the name implies, moles live an underground existence. They work secretly inside an enemy's intelligence service or top-secret facilities. They often work for their own country's intelligence agency but reveal confidential information to another country. The Mossad has a long history of recruiting moles who have access to data that Israel

wants and of setting up secret identities and fake companies for moles placed in enemy nations.

A double agent actually works for two different spy agencies. In most cases, a double agent is someone who has been caught spying for an enemy and coerced into sending back wrong intelligence, called disinformation. A double agent may also be a spy who decides to switch sides for money or because of a change in beliefs. An asset is a hidden source acting as a spy or providing secret information to a spy. Assets are very important to agencies such as the Mossad. They do the real undercover spying, while the Mossad agents often act as handlers, transmitting secret documents and photographs back to Israel and making sure the assets get paid for their work.

Right: Wolfgang Lotz was an illegal who worked undercover for the Mossad in the 1960s.

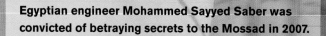

Egyptian engineer Mohammed Sayyed Saber was convicted of betraying secrets to the Mossad in 2007.

Some spies volunteer for the job. They may discover things going on that they believe should be revealed or stopped by supplying secret information. Men and women in the military may also volunteer to spy for their country, or they may become traitors and reveal secrets to an enemy. In general, agencies such as the Mossad do not accept volunteers. They recruit the agents they need within Israel or in other countries. That's how naval officer Victor Ostrovsky joined the Mossad.

In April 1979, Ostrovsky, a Canadian-born Israeli, received secret orders to attend a meeting at a military base near Tel Aviv. When he arrived, Ostrovsky was led into a small office where a stranger in civilian clothes told him, "We've pulled your name out of a computer; you fit our criteria. You are already serving your country, but there's a way you can serve it better. Are you interested?"

Ostrovsky said yes and began an intense period of recruitment and training. He described the process and his life as a Mossad agent in his 1990 book *By Way of Deception*. He also explained why he decided to leave the organization after several years when he realized that he disagreed with its methods and the actions of its leaders. Ultimately, he was not happy living the deceptive life of a spy for Israel.

As part of his recruitment process, Ostrovsky was questioned at length. The questions included: "Would you regard killing somebody for your country as something negative?" and "Is there anything more important than freedom?" Ostrovsky must have given the right answers because he soon began training to become a Mossad agent. He later learned that several thousand men and women had been interviewed to make up a training class of only 15 people.

Throughout the next two years, Ostrovsky and the other recruits were warned not to reveal anything about themselves to one another. They were even instructed to make up new names and to put together a believable new personal history. "Keep yourself to yourself," they were told. Recruits learned a variety of spy skills, or tradecraft. They learned how to code and decode messages; how to tail others and recognize when they were being followed; and how to use spy cameras, radio detection finding (RDF) equipment, and other secret instruments. Most of all, they learned how to blend in to get the information they wanted while avoiding detection. In other words, they learned how to live successfully in the shadows.

GO, GO GADGET

The purpose of espionage is to gather and transmit information that someone else wants kept secret. For most of human history, intelligence collection was done directly by individuals using deception and trickery and few other tools. In spy language, this is called HUMINT (human intelligence). In the 20th century, spies began using more technology to help them obtain information—from cameras to hidden microphones to `radio waves` to computers. For example, the Mossad and other spy agencies gather ELINT (electronic intelligence) via the Internet and computer monitoring or hacking; SIGINT (signal intelligence) by intercepting radio, telephone, and other communications; and PHOTINT (photographic intelligence) by studying photographs taken by spy planes, satellites, or human operatives. These methods fall under the heading of TECHINT (technical intelligence). Modern spies need a wide range of technical skills and support. Learning to use electronic gadgets has become an important part of their tradecraft.

MOSSAD

Because Israel is one of the world's leading countries in developing computers and electronic devices, the Mossad has a ready supply of high-tech tools at its disposal. One reported tool is a powerful computer program called Promis that is supposedly used to break into electronic systems around the world in order to uncover terrorist plots more successfully. Israel has never admitted to the existence of Promis, but its use has been reported by journalists who cover intelligence topics. These journalists have also reported that Israel has sold Promis systems to other countries in hopes of hacking into various security databases. Such reports have never been officially confirmed, however.

While TECHINT tools play a key role in the Mossad's work, simpler HUMINT tools also have their place. Miniature spy cameras enable Israeli operatives and moles to photograph secret actions or documents. Some of these cameras can be concealed in a spy's coat button, watch, or pen and operated via a wireless connection. Mossad agents also utilize small, sophisticated bugs, or listening devices. These usually contain a microphone, transmitter, and antenna. Once the bug is hidden

Even a container of motor oil can be used to camouflage electronic devices used by spies.

Technology in the form of miniature cameras plays a major role in the work of modern spies.

in a room or wired into a phone line, a spy can tune to a specific radio frequency to eavesdrop on a conversation or record a telephone call. It is even possible to bug someone's cell phone by sending a message with a computer virus attached that takes over the phone and allows the spy to monitor phone conversations and e-mails.

Modern spying often involves combining HUMINT and TECHINT to accomplish a goal. In a mission that took place from 2001 to 2007, American and Israeli spy agencies joined forces to achieve the desired results. (Because the U.S. views Israel as an important ally in its fight against terrorism, American intelligence agencies often cooperate with their Israeli counterparts.) The outcome of the mission was reported in several different media sources, with a detailed account provided by Salon.com in November 2009.

Starting in 2001, Mossad spies in Syria intercepted radio communications between military leaders in Syria and North Korea. They suspected that Syria was planning to develop nuclear weapons that might pose a threat to Israel. North Korea, which already

possessed nuclear weapons and technology, had previously sold Syria missiles and chemical weapons. Was Syria now looking to purchase nuclear technology from North Korea? Israel's intelligence community went on the alert.

Then, in 2004, electronic monitoring by the American National Security Agency (NSA) detected an unusual amount of telephone activity between North Korea and the Syrian desert town of Al Kibar. The Americans didn't listen in on the calls, but they notified Israeli intelligence officials, who then went into action. At that point, the dual forces of HUMINT and TECHINT really took over—helped by some luck, too.

In late 2006, Mossad spies tailed a Syrian government leader visiting London. They sneaked into his hotel room and installed a device in his laptop computer that allowed them to steal data. The spies found detailed plans and photographs showing construction of a possible nuclear reactor disguised to look like an ordinary factory. Warning bells went off in Israel.

The Mossad placed a mole inside the Al Kibar factory. This spy began electronically transmitting photographs and videos that showed what was really going on inside. The Israelis shared their

PANTHER

E-TOP

Machines called electric tethered observation platforms (foreground) can hover over areas to gather information.

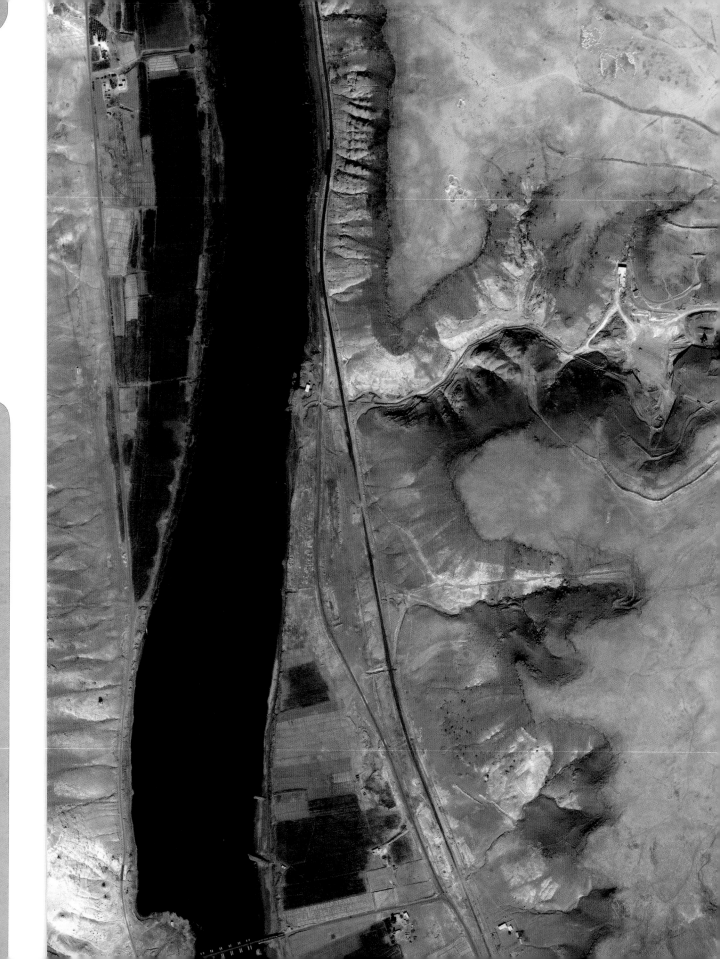

Opposite: Satellite images of Syria provided PHOTINT of the suspected nuclear reactor site.

findings with American intelligence and military leaders, who helped them determine exact coordinates for a possible bombing mission to destroy the site. (It should be noted that, throughout this time, Syrian officials denied the existence of any nuclear facilities in their country.)

Then a high-ranking Iranian military leader defected and agreed to tell members of the U.S. Central Intelligence Agency (CIA) what he knew about Iran's nuclear plans. He revealed that Iran was helping to fund a secret nuclear facility in Syria. The CIA passed the defector's information along to the Mossad.

Still, Israel felt it needed more proof before taking action to destroy the Syrian plant. Using low-flying helicopters to avoid radar detection, a team of technicians was flown into Syria to take soil samples to check for radiation in the Al Kibar area. They narrowly avoided capture by a

Syrian patrol. Meanwhile, other spies reported that a North Korean ship was sailing toward Syria with suspicious-looking pipes on board that could be used to build a reactor and that another ship would arrive soon with a cargo of uranium materials. This was all the evidence Israeli leaders felt they needed; they decided to act. Late on the night of September 5, 2007, ten Israeli aircraft took to the air, flying west over the Mediterranean. They seemed to be on a routine patrolling mission until seven planes peeled off and flew over Syria. With the bombing coordinates already programmed into their computers, the pilots flew over Al Kibar and wiped out the nuclear reactor, then flew home at top speed.

Surprisingly, the bombing mission did not arouse much anger. Instead, the Syrians quickly cleaned up the debris and paved over the area so that no one, least of all United Nations weapons inspectors, could tell what had existed there before. It would be nearly two years before the story of Israel's spy work and bombing came to light.

ISRAELI SPIES AND SPYMASTERS

Spies need to know how to see without being seen and how to uncover secrets while revealing little about themselves. No one was more secretive than Isser Harel, Israel's first spymaster. Harel immigrated to Palestine from Latvia in 1930 when he was 18. He showed his talent for espionage even then by smuggling a revolver past British military agents. They never suspected that the small (4-foot-8), innocent-looking young man might be hiding a weapon. Over the years, many of Israel's enemies would underestimate the talents and determination of "Isser the Little."

In the late 1930s, Harel joined the intelligence wing of the Haganah, the Jewish underground army in Palestine, spying on the British forces occupying Palestine. In 1948, Harel was asked to organize and lead Shin Bet, the internal security service, and then to become director of the Mossad in 1952, where he served until 1963. During those years, none of Harel's friends and neighbors knew exactly what he did for a living. His secretive nature became legendary. His

MOSSAD

colleagues told a joke about a taxi ride he once took. When the driver asked Harel where he wanted to go, Harel replied, "I can't tell you. It's a secret."

Israeli intelligence was not Harel's only passion. He also had an intense desire to capture Nazi war criminals who had fled Germany after World War II. In 1957, he received reliable evidence that Adolf Eichmann, the suspected mastermind behind the Nazi plan to kill all European Jews, was living under a new name in Argentina. Harel devised a meticulous plan to locate Eichmann, capture him, and bring him back to Israel for a public trial. The mission took three years to complete successfully, and capturing Eichmann became the crowning achievement of Harel's spy career.

While Harel was a spymaster in Israel, two of his most important operatives were living dangerous undercover lives in enemy countries. The information provided by both men would be vital to Israel's lightning-quick victory over Egypt and Syria in the 1967 Six-Day War—though one would be executed and the other imprisoned by the time hostilities broke out.

Eli Cohen was an Egyptian-born Jew who could easily pass for an

Israeli General Ariel Sharon (right) and defense minister Moshe Dayan (left) in October 1973.

EVOLUTION OF ESPIONAGE
A Deadly Disagreement

Aman and Mossad leaders do not always agree on what is needed for Israel's security. One disagreement proved deadly in the fall of 1973. Reports had been coming in to both agencies about military buildups by Egypt and Syria. Aman leaders were certain neither country would start a war; Mossad leaders believed just the opposite. While the military stood down, Mossad chief Zvi Zamir went on a fact-finding mission to Europe. What he learned worried him. He sent a frantic message back to Israel, but he was too late. Arab troops were already crossing the Israeli border on the holiest day of the Jewish year, Yom Kippur. The Yom Kippur War had begun.

The Syrian capital of Damascus is one of the oldest continuously inhabited cities in the world.

Arab. In 1955, Cohen traveled to Israel and volunteered to become a spy. He worked first for Aman and then for the Mossad. Needing an operative in Syria, the Mossad sent Cohen for training in Argentina, where he built an elaborate legend as a Syrian businessman named Kamal Amin Ta'abet. Many wealthy Syrians were living in Argentina in the late 1950s, and Cohen/Ta'abet befriended them. He built up trust and received letters of introduction to powerful people in Damascus, Syria, where he moved in 1962.

In Damascus, the Mossad helped Cohen set up a fake textile import/export business, and he began sending goods throughout Europe. The seemingly prosperous businessman was soon invited to gatherings of Syrian political and military leaders and even went on tours of several Syrian military bases. He set up a radio transmitter in his apartment and sent out Morse code messages relating details of the Syrian military setup. He also took pictures, which he transferred to microfilm, and made copies of top-secret documents on Syrian troop movements and locations of warplanes. He hid the evidence in hollowed-out legs of pieces of furniture he shipped to Mossad drops.

Over time, Cohen became careless, though. He often made his radio transmissions at the same time every evening. The radio activity was discovered by Syrian security using RDF equipment, and Cohen was captured. He was given two choices: become a double agent or be tried and hanged. He took the second choice and was executed in 1965 before a cheering crowd in Damascus. Still, the Syrian military secrets he uncovered would prove invaluable two years later.

Wolfgang Lotz was a German-born Jew who came to Palestine to escape the Nazis. He fought with the British against the Germans in Egypt during World War II, where he mastered Arabic and English as well as German and Hebrew. The Mossad approached him about becoming a spy in Egypt. "I was blond and stocky and the very epitome of an ex-German officer," he explained. Lotz was sent to Germany for training and to help establish his legend as an ex-Nazi who wanted to set up a horse ranch in Egypt. Then, in 1960, he moved to Cairo.

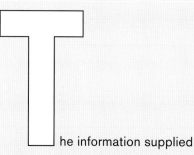
Below: Israel made use of tanks to roll into Syria during the Six-Day War in June 1967.

Like Cohen, Lotz befriended important political and military leaders. Once, he was taken on a tour of an Egyptian missile facility where his guide said, "The Israelis have an excellent intelligence service. They must not learn about our rockets until we strike a blow with them. Now, let me show you around."

Lotz telegraphed reports to Tel Aviv and made several trips to Paris to meet with his Mossad contacts. Then he, too, became sloppy, and his radio transmissions were detected by Egyptian security in February 1965. He was arrested but protested that he was not Jewish and was spying only for the money. He was sent to prison and later returned to Israel as part of a prisoner exchange.

The information supplied by Cohen and Lotz helped the Israeli military learn just where to strike the most devastating blows against Syria and Egypt. When war broke out among the three countries in June 1967, Israel

EVOLUTION OF ESPIONAGE
Codename: Operation Sphinx

In the late 1970s, Israel became convinced that Iraq was building a nuclear weapons factory near Baghdad. The Mossad began a secret campaign to make sure the factory never became operational. Nicknamed Operation Sphinx, the campaign included the recruitment of an Iraqi nuclear scientist working in France as a mole, a series of bombings at French and Italian factories supplying Iraq with parts for its reactor, and even an unsolved murder of an Egyptian nuclear scientist helping the Iraqis. Then, late one night in June 1981, Israeli fighter planes flew a 684-mile (1,100 km) mission to Iraq (called Operation Babylon) and destroyed the plant, setting back Iraq's nuclear capabilities by many years.

Ten years after his arrest, convicted spy Jonathan Pollard was granted Israeli citizenship.

struck quickly inside its enemies' territory, declaring victory a mere six days later.

Two of Israel's most controversial spies were American citizens working for the U.S. armed forces. During the 1980s, they provided Israel with classified documents concerning American military plans in the Middle East. The men, Jonathan Pollard and Ben-Ami Kadish, reported to the same Israeli handler in the U.S. Both men felt their spying activities were justified because Israel was an American ally and would not use the information to harm the U.S. American leaders disagreed, arguing that the spying had had a serious impact on U.S. security. Pollard was captured in 1985 and subsequently sentenced to life imprisonment. Kadish, though long suspected, was not charged with spying until 2008. He pled guilty but was fined rather than jailed because of his poor health.

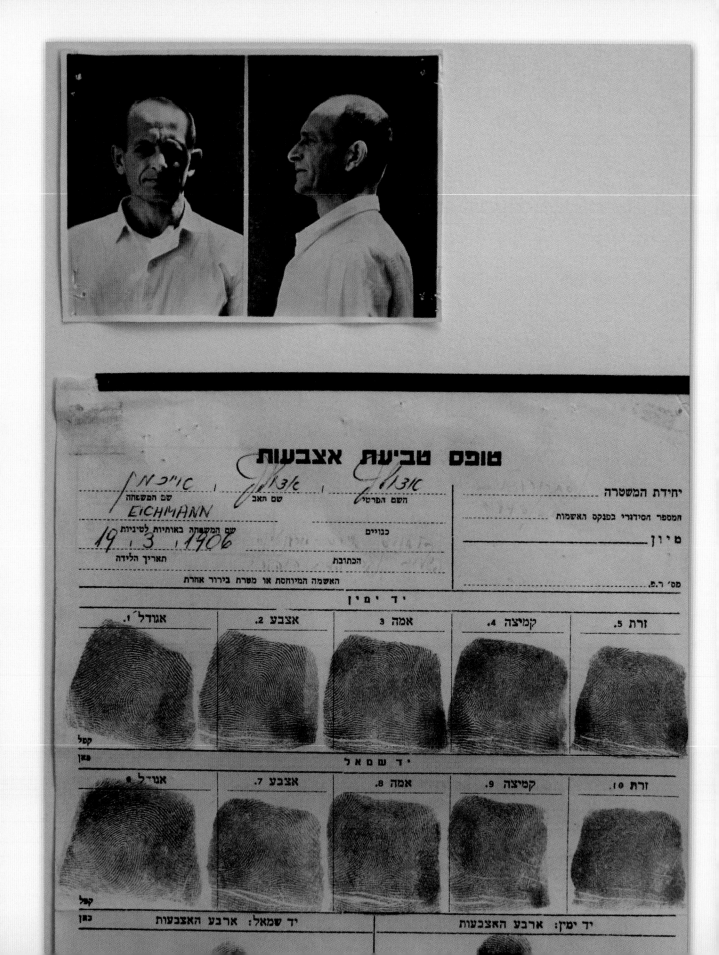

טופס טביעת אצבעות

יחידת המשטרה			
מספר הסידורי בפנקס האשמות			
מיון			
מס׳ ר.פ.			

השם הפרטי	שם האב	שם משפחה
אייכמן		EICHMANN
כנויים		שם המשפחה באותיות לטיניות
הכתובת		תאריך הלידה 19 . 3 . 1906
האשמה המיוחסת או משרת בירור אחרת		

יד ימין

אגודל 1.	אצבע 2.	אמה 3	קמיצה 4.	זרת 5.
קפל				
כאן				

יד שמאל

אגודל 6.	אצבע 7.	אמה 8.	קמיצה 9.	זרת 10.
קפל				
כאן				

יד שמאל: ארבע האצבעות	יד ימין: ארבע האצבעות

MISSIONS POSSIBLE

Some of the missions that Mossad agents have carried out seem more like movie scripts than real-life drama. In fact, several of them have been made into exciting movies. For example, *The House on Garibaldi Street* (1979) is based on Isser Harel's account of how Mossad agents captured Adolf Eichmann in Argentina and smuggled him out of South America to stand trial in Israel. It took more than two years to locate Eichmann, who suspected he was being hunted and moved with his family several times to avoid capture. Finally, on May 11, 1960, he was grabbed in broad daylight while getting off a bus near his home on Garibaldi Street in Buenos Aires. Then he was taken to a secret location, where agents checked for Nazi tattoos and other characteristics that verified his identity.

Eichmann was kept closely guarded for 10 days. Meanwhile, a Mossad agent was planted in a local hospital, supposedly suffering from a brain injury. After a week of treatment by a doctor

employed by the Mossad, the "patient" was released and given permission to fly home the next day on an El Al plane. Eichmann's photograph quickly replaced the agent's on a fake passport, and he was disguised with bandages and rushed past airport security and onboard the plane. Within days, the world learned of Eichmann's capture, and Argentine leaders expressed great anger. But the mission had been accomplished. Eichmann was later tried and executed for his crimes.

The 2005 movie *Munich*,

Opposite: Adolf Eichmann's police file was donated to Jerusalem's Yad Vashem, a Holocaust memorial museum, in 2005.

directed by Steven Spielberg, focuses on one of the most controversial missions Mossad agents ever carried out. The movie opens with the shocking massacre of 11 Israeli athletes and coaches by terrorists at the 1972 Summer Olympics in Munich, Germany. How Israel responded to the massacre is at the heart of the movie. Following the direct orders of Israeli prime minister Golda Meir, a Mossad "hit squad" was dispatched to hunt down and assassinate 12 members of the terrorist group Black September that had carried out the murders. Israel was

Below: Six of the 11 Israeli hostages killed by Black September terrorists in 1972 are shown.

seeking revenge, not justice.

Slightly more than a month after the Olympics, the first terrorist was gunned down in the lobby of his apartment building in Rome, Italy. Then, over the next 6 years, 11 other identified terrorists were killed through a variety of methods. Several were shot by guns equipped with silencers fired from cars or fast-moving motorcycles. Others were killed in their apartments by remote-controlled bombs detonated by a telephone call and a radio transmission.

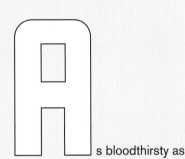

As bloodthirsty as these killings were, the Mossad might have escaped major public outcry, except for a huge mistake made in Lillehammer, Norway, in July 1973. Following a tip, a Mossad team arrived in Lillehammer, where it tracked down and then executed the suspected leader of the Munich terrorists. The victim strongly resembled the man they had seen in photographs, but, as it turns out, he was actually a Moroccan waiter in the wrong place at the wrong time. The

mistake quickly came to light, and five members of the Mossad team were arrested by Norwegian police before they could flee the country. All were given relatively light sentences for the murder, but the damage done to the Mossad's reputation was significant. Nations around the world condemned Israel's actions, and other intelligence agencies scoffed at the Mossad's poor spy work.

An amazing Israeli spy and rescue mission several years later received much more positive response from people around the world. It is the focus of the exciting 1977 movie *Raid on Entebbe.* The events took place in late June and early July of 1976 in the east-central African nation of Uganda. At the time, Uganda was run by a dictator named Idi Amin, who gave support

One terrorist stood guard on the balcony of the Olympic athletes' housing complex.

Below: On July 5, 1976, the hostages who were French returned to Paris, while others remained in Entebbe.

to many terrorist groups.

On June 27, a group of terrorists took over an Air France plane flying from Israel to Paris with 250 passengers and crew aboard. They forced the pilot to fly to the Entebbe airport in Uganda. There, all non-Jews were released and flown back to Israel, but 105 Jewish hostages were kept under close guard inside the airport terminal. The terrorists said they would kill the hostages unless 53 terrorists were freed from jails in Israel and elsewhere by July 4. Israeli prime minister Yitzhak Rabin pretended that Israel would negotiate with the terrorists as a trick to buy time to undertake a rescue mission.

Mossad spies based in Africa studied airport blueprints, handled all preparations needed for the rescue party, and made sure no one in Uganda suspected that a raid was in the works. Other agents interviewed freed hostages to learn more about the airport setup. Meanwhile, Israeli military and intelligence leaders organized the operation. Approximately 200 soldiers would have to be flown nearly 8 hours in cargo planes, land without being detected, get inside the terminal where the hostages were being held, wipe out the terrorists before they could shoot any hostages, rush the hostages onto the plane, and

EVOLUTION OF ESPIONAGE
Tracking a Terrorist

During the 1990s, as the relationship between Palestinians and Jews in Israel became increasingly hostile, stopping terrorism became the major focus of Shin Bet, Israel's internal security agency. One important Shin Bet case involved the tracking, interrogation, and arrest of a Palestinian doctor named Hassan Khawaja. Shin Bet agents had grown suspicious of a series of trips that Khawaja had made to Lebanon, Algeria, Syria, Iran, and Turkey. He was arrested in 1996 as he returned from one of his trips. Under questioning, Khawaja admitted that he had received military training and was helping form an organization in Gaza that was designed to carry out deadly attacks on Jews.

EVOLUTION OF ESPIONAGE
A Busy Year

In one year, 2007, several Middle Eastern Arab countries suffered serious—and mysterious—setbacks in their efforts to possess nuclear and chemical weapons. A nuclear plant under construction in Syria was bombed. An explosion at a chemical weapons factory in Syria killed dozens of skilled technicians. A convoy of trucks delivering weapons from Iran to the extremist militant group Hezbollah in Lebanon was blown up before it crossed the Iranian border. Puzzling malfunctions began occurring in nuclear facilities in Iran. No one claimed responsibility for any of these events, but all were probably the work of Mossad operatives intent on protecting Israel from its enemies.

take off for Israel. The mission leaders gave themselves only one hour to carry out the raid itself. Any more time would give Amin's army time to attack the rescuers. A full-scale rehearsal was held in Israel to get the timing right, then the mission was a go.

Amazingly, the raid at Entebbe took exactly 58 minutes and resulted in only 4 Israeli casualties—3 hostages died in the gunfire that ensued, and the leader of the mission was killed by a Ugandan sentry as he led the hostages to the plane. The daring rescue was a perfect example of how spies and military leaders could work together to combat terrorism successfully.

The Eichmann capture, Munich revenge plot, and Entebbe rescue mission all illustrate the independence and determination of Israel's intelligence community. They also show that the tiny Middle Eastern country is willing to take a lot of risks to do things its own way. Some mistakes have been made, and Israel has often been accused of being reckless by other countries—even by its closest ally, the U.S. Israel's leaders do not seem concerned by the criticism. They believe that, in order to protect a country surrounded by large, powerful nations intent on its destruction, they can't always play by the rules.

**Above: Iran's Bushehr nuclear power plant was
launched at full capacity in the spring of 2012.**

ENDNOTES

agents–people who work for, but are not necessarily officially employed by, an intelligence service

Arab–describing a person living in an Arabic-speaking country in the Middle East or North Africa; most Arabs are Muslims who practice the religion of Islam

concentration camps–places where large numbers of people are imprisoned and forced to labor or await execution

covert operations–undercover or hidden activities

defected–in the context of spying, chose to leave the control of one country's intelligence service to work for another country; defectors often provide vital information to their new country

drones–unmanned aircraft, often directed by remote control, that are used to take secret photographs of or attack targets

drops–secure locations that usually include a sealed container where spies and their handlers can exchange information or intelligence materials to avoid meeting in person

embassy–the headquarters of an ambassador and staff in a foreign country

extremist–describing a person or group with political or religious views that are extreme, or radical

handlers–case officers who are responsible for recruiting and directing agents and assets working in a country

intelligence–information uncovered and transmitted by a spy

neutralizing–taking actions to destroy or counter the effectiveness of a spy or the intelligence supplied by a spy

nuclear–relating to or involving weapons using nuclear energy such as bombs, rockets, and other destructive measures

operatives–undercover agents working for an intelligence agency

propaganda–material distributed to promote a government's or group's point of view or to damage an opposing point of view; some propaganda is untrue or unfairly exaggerated

radio detection finding (RDF) equipment–electronic equipment that is able to monitor and locate the source of radio transmissions; it is often used to catch spies

radio waves–electromagnetic waves that carry radio signals and are used for communication

reconnoiter–to inspect or study something, often secretly, in order to obtain information

tail–someone following a spy who is acting undercover

tradecraft–the procedures, techniques, and devices used by spies to carry out their activities

war criminal–a person who violates international laws or customs concerning warfare; war criminals are often accused of mistreating civilians and prisoners

Yom Kippur War–a 1973 conflict among Israel and several Arab nations that began on the Jewish holy day of Yom Kippur, lasted for 20 days, and cost more than 2,500 Israeli lives; it is known in Arab nations as the October War

WEB SITES

The Institute for Intelligence and Special Operations
http://www.mossad.gov.il//Eng/AboutUs.aspx
Learn more about the Mossad directly from its Web site.

Israeli Security Agency: Famous Cases
http://www.shabak.gov.il/English/History/Affairs/Pages/default.aspx
Discover all the details known about Shin Bet's most storied intelligence operations.

SELECTED BIBLIOGRAPHY

Ben-Hanan, Eli. *Our Man in Damascus: Elie Cohen*. New York: Crown Publishers, 1969.

Coleman, Janet Wyman. *Secrets, Lies, Gizmos, and Spies: A History of Spies and Espionage*. New York: Abrams Books for Young Readers, 2006.

Eisenberg, Dennis, Uri Dan, and Eli Landau. *The Mossad: Inside Stories*. New York: Paddington Press, 1978.

Hastedt, Glenn. *Espionage: A Reference Handbook*. Santa Barbara, Calif.: ABC-CLIO, 2003.

Ostrovsky, Victor, and Clair Hoy. *By Way of Deception: The Making and Unmaking of a Mossad Officer*. New York: St. Martin's Press, 1990.

Owen, David. *Spies: The Undercover World of Secrets, Gadgets, and Lies*. Buffalo, N.Y.: Firefly Books, 2004.

Pollath, Erick, and Holger Stark. "How Israel destroyed Syria's Al Kibar nuclear reactor." *Salon*, November 3, 2009, http://www.salon.com/news/feature/2009/11/03/syria_israel.

Raviv, Dan, and Yossi Melman. *Every Spy a Prince: The Complete History of Israel's Intelligence Community*. Boston: Houghton Mifflin, 1990.

INDEX